一条石板路　　千年磁器口

A slabstone road has witnessed a thousand years' history of Ciqikou

磁器口古镇风情
Customs and Practices of the Ancient Town Ciqikou

鲁 钝　况向军　绘图
木　文　撰文

Sketched by Lu Dun & Kuang Xiangjun
Noted by Mu Wen

学苑出版社　重庆磁器口古镇管理委员会监制
Academy Press　Supervised by Chongqing Ciqikou Municipal Commission

图书在版编目（CIP）数据

磁器口古镇风情 / 鲁钝 等绘画撰文 . －－ 北京 : 学苑出版社，2019.7

ISBN 978-7-5077-5734-7

Ⅰ．①磁… Ⅱ．①鲁… Ⅲ．①乡镇－概况－重庆 Ⅳ．① K927.19

中国版本图书馆 CIP 数据核字 (2019) 第 123125 号

责任编辑：杨　雷　陈柯宇
出版发行：学苑出版社
社　　址：北京市丰台区南方庄 2 号院 1 号楼
邮政编码：100079
网　　址：www.book001.com
电子信箱：xueyuanpress@163.com
联系电话：010-67601101（销售部）　67603091（总编室）
经　　销：新华书店
印　刷　厂：河北赛文印刷有限公司
开本尺寸：889×1194　1/24
印　　张：6.5
字　　数：100 千字
版　　次：2019 年 9 月北京第 1 版
印　　次：2019 年 9 月第 1 次印刷
定　　价：88.00 元

目　录

历史遗迹　Historical Site ／ 1

磁器口的由来　Origin of Ciqikou / 4

龙隐传说　Legend of the Hidden Dragon / 6

龙隐门牌坊　Longyin Memorial Archway / 8

少妇尿童雕塑　Young Married Woman and the Pissing Child / 10

码头繁华　Prosperous Scene of the Ciqikou Port / 12

修建钟家院　Innovation of Family Zhong's Courtyard / 14

翰林院的举子　Candidates of Hanlin Academy / 16

重庆抗战军人子女教养院　Chongqing Nursing Institute for the Children of Military Men Fighting in the War of Resistance against Japan / 18

丁肇中入读磁器口小学　Samuel Chao Chung Ting Enrolled in Ciqikou Elementary School / 20

华子良脱险　"Hua Ziliang" Escaping from White Residence and Zhazi Cave Prison / 22

荣强牙科诊所　Rongqiang Dental Clinic / 24

徐悲鸿创作《巴人汲水图》　Xu Beihong Creating the *Water-Drawing Graph of People from Chongqing and Sichuan* / 26

张书旂创作《百鸽图》　Zhang Shuqi Creating the *White Pigeons Painting* / 28

七七电影院　July 7th Cinema / 30

自然地理与建筑　Geography & Architecture　/　35

嘉陵江　Jialing River / 38

凤凰山　Phoenix Mountain / 40

金碧山　Jinbi Mountain / 42

马鞍山　Ma'an Mountain / 44

凤凰溪　Phoenix Creek / 46

清水溪　Qingshui Creek / 48

九石缸河滩　Nine Stone Jars Benchland / 50

古渡口　Ancient Ferry / 52

凤凰寺　Phoenix Temple / 54

宝轮寺　Baolun Temple / 56

宝轮寺·大雄宝殿　Great Buddha's Hall of Baolun Temple / 58

宝善宫　Baoshangong Taoist Temple / 60

宝善宫·古井　Ancient Well in Baoshangong Taoist Temple / 62

深水井　Shenshui Well (Deep Well) / 64

文昌宫古寨遗址　Historic Site of Wenchanggong Taoist Temple / 66

太平桥　Taiping Bridge / 68

双龙桥　Shuanglong Bridge / 70

仁寿桥　Renshou Bridge / 72

古旧民居　Architectural Complex of Folk Houses / 74

青石老街　Bluestone Ancient Street / 78

高石坎　High Stone Ladder / 82

磁正街　Ciqikou Main Street / 84

磁横街　Ciqikou Side Street / 86

翰林院　Hanlin Academy / 88

鑫记杂货店　Grocery Store of the Xin's / 90

钟家院　The Zhong's Courtyard / 92

童家院子　The Tong's Courtyard / 94

江防碉堡　Jiangfang Pillbox (the Pillbox along Yangtze River) / 96

架高来石刻　Stone Carving of "*Jia Gao Lai*" (three Chinese Characters to warn boats that the water is deep and flow is rapid ahead) / 98

小重庆碑　Little Chongqing Stele / 100

抗日阵亡将士纪念碑　Cenotaph for Sacrificed Officers and Soldiers in the War of Resistance against Japan / 102

四川省立教育学院旧址　Site of Sichuan Provincial Education College / 104

井中天茶坊　Jingzhongtian (which literally means Sky in the Well) Tea House / 106

聚森茂酱园　Jusenmao Sauce and Pickles Shop / 108

风土人情　Local Customs and Practices　/　113

揽载帮 好吃船　Offering Food and Beverage for Boatmen / 116

庙会　Temple Fair / 118

舞龙　Playing the Dragon / 120

坝坝茶　Baba Tea / 122

金钱板　Jinqian Plate (Small Rhythm Instrument made of Bamboo Plate with Copper Coin inlaid at the Upper End of the Bamboo Plate) / 124

莲花闹　Lianhuanao Opera (a Popular Folk Art Form which literally means the Lotus Noise) / 126

花轿迎亲　Welcoming Bride by Bridal Sedan Chair / 128

椒盐花生　Peanut Mixed with Spicy Salt / 130

毛血旺　Maoxuewang (Chongqing Style Boiled Blood Curd) / 132

红汤火锅　Hot Pot of Red Soup / 134

黄粑糕制作技艺　Manufacturing Workmanship of Yellow Rice Cake / 136

陈麻花制作技艺　Manufacturing Workmanship of Fried Dough Twist of Family Chen / 138

聚森茂酱油制作技艺　Manufacturing Workmanship of Jusenmao Soy Sauce / 140

千张制作技艺　Manufacturing Workmanship of Qianzhang (Dried Pieces of Bean Curd) / 142

历史遗迹
Historical Site

磁器口古镇在明代中期就逐渐形成水陆交会的商业码头，到清末民初，更是"白日里千人拱手，入夜后万盏明灯"，从大码头到童家桥，沿街商户千余家，古镇内外作坊林立。抗战全面爆发，重庆成为中国的战时首都，众多的国府机关、高等院校迁来磁器口一带，形成著名的沙磁文化区。磁器口古镇作为沙磁文化区的中心，文化、工业、商贸、交通的繁荣达到鼎盛。

青瓦在浓绿的树荫下、竹摇椅冰顺凉滑、一小杯热热的坝坝茶……在磁器口古旧民居的宁静小院子里，感受木、石、砖围合下的空间，仿佛时光倒流，可以做一个从唐宋到今日的素雅清淡的梦。

走在青石板路上，看看江中水流里的船，闻闻小巷子里飘荡的麻辣浓香，听听沿街窗口传出的摆龙门阵的大嗓门吧……

The grey tiles are under the deep green tree shade; the rocking chair made of bamboo is pleasantly cool and smooth; a cup of warm tea in the bowl with fitted cover diffuses coziness...in the small tranquil courtyard among the ancient dwelling houses in Ciqikou. Feeling the space circumvented by wood, rock and brick, the simplicity but elegance seem to reverse the times, in which a dream from the Tang and Song Dynasties to present could be dreamed.

Walking on the road made of blue stone plate, seeing the boats floating in stream, smelling the aroma flying in alley, hearing the loud voice of gossip out of the windows along the street.

磁器口的由来　Origin of Ciqikou

中国西南山区的"场"多指山间平地。大约在公元1000年前后的宋代,磁器口一带名白崖场,白崖场有座白崖寺。明朝初年白崖寺已名宝轮寺,相传明建文帝曾在此隐匿数年。后宝轮寺改名为龙隐寺,白崖场相应改称为龙隐场。

清代时,龙隐场日渐繁华,尤以瓷器生产名声大噪。民国时则成为嘉陵江中上游的商品集散之地,曾有每日300多艘货船进出的记录,大宗货物就是瓷器。渐渐地人们把龙隐镇叫成瓷器口,而后又把"瓷"字写成了"磁"字。于是,龙隐之名便悄悄隐没在老人们的故事里;"磁器口"则名声远扬至今日。

In about 1000, Ciqikou and its vicinity was named as Baiyachang (which literally means the White Cliff Rural Market). In Baiya Chang, there is a temple named Baiya Temple. It's a question beyond our knowledge that the name of the rural market originated from the name of the temple or vice versa.

According to legend, in the early years of the Ming Dynasty (1368 ~ 1644 A.D.), Emperor Jianwen sought for asylum in the Baolun Temple (or Baiya Temple) of the Baiyachang for several years. Subsequently, the Baolun Temple was renamed as the Longyin Temple (the Temple of the Hidden Dragon), and the Baiya Rural Market was renamed as the Longyin Rural Market accordingly. In the Qing Dynasty (1644 ~ 1911 A.D.), the Longyin Rural Market became increasingly prosperous and was especially famous for its ceramic production. In the era of the Republic of China (1912 ~ 1949 A.D.), the Longyin Rural Market became the distributing center of goods in the upper reach area of the Jialing River.

磁器口的由来
Origin of Ciqikou

龙隐传说　Legend of the Hidden Dragon

1398 年，明朝开国皇帝朱元璋传位给皇孙朱允炆，是为建文帝。当时，建文帝的叔叔、权力最大的燕王朱棣以"清君侧"之名包围了皇宫，皇宫大火后建文帝便下落不明。《明史》对建文帝的失踪给出了三种说法：阖宫自焚、流亡海外、逊国为僧。寻找建文帝，又衍生出很多历史事件。

建文帝曾隐藏在磁器口的传说在重庆一带非常盛行，而且重庆南泉的建文峰、渝中的龙隐路、渝北的御临河、巴南的圣灯山等都相传和建文帝有关。不过，历史之谜终究是一团麻，磁器口（龙隐场）的不断繁华倒是真实的。

In 1398, Zhu Yuanzhang, the founding Emperor of the Ming Dynasty (1368 ～ 1644 A.D.) passed on the throne to his royal grandson Zhu Yunwen, as Emperor Jianwen. Soon after ascending the throne, the new Emperor took steps to weaken the power of each seignior. Zhu Di (also known as King Yan), who was Emperor Jianwen's uncle and held the greatest power among all seigniors, surrounded the Imperial Palace in the name of "riding the Emperor of 'evil' ministers". Consequently, Emperor Jianwenset fire to the Imperial Palace before disappearing without a trace. Some said that Emperor Jianwen sought for asylum in the Baiya Temple, and the legend has been very popular in the Chongqing City. However, the historical mystery remains a confusing myth, and the growing prosperity of Ciqikou (Longyin Rural Market) has been a indisputable fact.

龙隐传说
Legend of the Hidden Dragon

龙隐门牌坊　Longyin Memorial Archway

相传，当年建文帝为势所逼，不得不离开隐居五年的磁器口（白崖场）。临行时，他坐在码头前，只闻百鸟展翅，滚滚逝水东流去，睹物思己，不禁潸然泪下。真龙天子的泪，自非凡物，那泪落地不败，却慢慢凝结，化作一支玉笔，晶莹剔透，似有生机。见泪化笔，建文帝心中怅然。一国之君，理当以社稷昌盛、国奉民安为重。何以争位？遂提笔疾书"劝君莫话封侯事，一将功成万骨枯。明明孰胜汉唐景，祥和天道似可期"，写罢黯然离去。后人将建文帝高去之处修筑牌坊，曰：龙隐门。

In according to legend, Emperor Jianwen was forced to leave Baiyachang where he lived in seclusion for five years. Upon leaving, he wrote down something without hesitation before leaving. At the place where Emperor Jianwen left, later generations built a memorial archway called the Longyin Gate.

龙隐门牌坊
Longyin Memorial Archway

少妇尿童雕塑
Young Married Woman and the Pissing Child

　　磁器口有个古老的传说。说建文帝避难磁器口时病了，终日咳嗽。他又不敢找郎中看病买药，他叔叔永乐皇帝正差人到处找他呢。一天晚上，痛苦不堪的建文帝梦见神仙让他喝一点儿童子尿，说这样你的病便会好了。落难的凤凰不如鸡，建文帝第二天便出庙暗寻童子尿。走到宝轮寺旁，刚好见一少妇抱着小男孩在屙尿。建文帝手持缘钵说明来意，一碗童子尿喝下去，病症一扫而光。后来人们才知道那个讨尿的和尚居然就是真龙天子建文帝，于是便管童子尿叫"护龙水"了。

In Ciqikou, there was an ancient legend. Emperor Jianwen was sick when he sought for asylum in Ciqikou. At that time, he coughed all day long and suffered from refractory rheumatism. He was afraid to see the doctor and buy medicine, because his uncle, Emperor Yongle was sending people to search for him at that time.One night, the anguished Emperor Jianwen dreamed of a celestial being, who told the Emperor to drink the urine of a child of 7 years old and assured him of recovery. The next day, the Emperor went out of the temple to seek for the urine of child. After drinking a bowl of urine, he was fully recovered from his disease.

少妇尿童雕塑

Young Married Woman and the Pissing Child

码头繁华　Prosperous Scene of the Ciqikou Port

　　清代中叶，磁器口的水陆港口贸易达到极盛。除瓷器贸易外，磁器口还有牛市、猪市、铁货市场、木材市场、竹子市场等，其港口成为嘉陵江下游最大的物资集散地。民国年间，大批文化教育单位迁居到磁器口以及周边地区，磁器口商贸活动更加繁荣，码头边的河滩上还修建了简易的军事机场。

　　曾几何时，磁器口有"白日里千人拱手，入夜后万盏明灯"的繁盛，被赞誉为"小重庆"。

In the middle years of the Qing Dynasty, the trade through waterways, land transport and port in Ciqikou reached its peak. In the years of the Republic of China, as the National Government relocated the capital to the Chongqing City, a large amount of cultural and educational entities moved to Ciqikou and the peripheral areas. As a result, the cultural business of Ciqikou commenced to thrive for a long time accordingly.

码头繁华
Prosperous Scene of the Ciqikou Port

修建钟家院　Innovation of Family Zhong's Courtyard

　　磁器口古镇黄桷坪1巷17号,是一所兼具南北建筑风格的大院子。院子的主人钟云亭,清代人士,他曾是清代北京紫禁城内务府的宫廷采办,据说因为办差有功曾得过慈禧太后的封赏。

　　大约在1880年,钟云亭告老还乡,先在北京请人设计好图纸,然后回到故乡磁器口给自己家修了一栋大宅子。北方的图纸、南方的工匠,所以钟家院既有北方四合院的格局,天井宽敞、轴线对称严谨;又有南方民居的精致典雅,房顶建材使用小青瓦,建筑结构为穿逗房;更有巴渝民间独特的建筑技艺。

　　钟家院现已辟为清代民居展示场所,基本恢复了昔日风貌。

This is a courtyard that manifests the blend of both the southern and northern styles of architecture. The owner of the courtyard Zhong Yunting resigned from office and returned to his native town in about 1880. He asked the designers to make the design drawing in Beijing firstly, and then went to his hometown Ciqikou to build a big house. The blending of the drawings of north and the craftsmen of south offered a mixed style for Family Zhong's Courtyard. Therefore, Family Zhong's Courtyard does not only have the pattern of quadrangle courtyard typical in North China, but also the delicacy of folk house in South China, and even the unique folk construction techniques of Chongqing and Sichuan.

修建钟家院
Innovation of Family Zhong's Courtyard

翰林院的举子　Candidates of Hanlin Academy

　　翰林，是中国古代的官名，翰林院，用现在的语言描述，可以算把翰林们集中在一起办公的机构，其设置是从唐代开始的。朝各代，翰林学士始终是社会中地位最高的群体之一，科考入翰林院，便成为古代很多人的人生目标。

　　磁器口也有一个被称作翰林院的地方，原为清代建的鲤石学舍。位于磁器口黄桷坪的鲤石学舍恐怕是今重庆主城保留下来的仅有的古代私塾了。学舍为清乾隆时期孙姓人所开，学舍培养出三个举人、两个翰林，故有"一门三举子，五里两翰林"之说。目前，该院落仅存正房三间，全由水桶粗的上好柏树穿逗成房屋骨架，一般民居颇为少见。院中小拜月台、院旁大拜月台遗迹仍然存在，仿佛在向人诉说该院昔日的辉煌。

Hanlin is the title of a type of officials in the ancient times of China. There is a former site of Hanlin Academy which was the old-style private school launched by Sun Wenzhi. Among the students out of this academy, there are three men with the family name of Sun who were selected as Juren (the successful candidates of the imperial examinations at provincial level), and two other men were selected as Jinshi (the successful candidates in the highest imperial examinations).Subsequently, both the two successful candidates in the highest imperial examinations assumed official positions in the Hanlin Academy. Therefore, people called this place as the former residence of Hanlin officials, and this place won the reputation of "Three-Juren of the Same First Name, Two-Hanlin in Neighbor Community."

翰林院的举子
Candidates of Hanlin Academy

重庆抗战军人子女教养院
Chongqing Nursing Institute for the Children of Military Men Fighting in the War of Resistance against Japan

  重庆抗战军人子女教养院,是中华慈幼协会于 1939 年 9 月在磁器口石子山创设的。专招收"抗战军人子女",是当时全国各地零星分布的抗战军人子女教养院中的一所。
  该教养院下设总务股、文书股、会计股、庶务股、教务股、养护股、卫生股、童军训练股、生活训练股、服务训练股、生产训练股、幼童部等机构部门。

In September 1939, the "Chongqing Nursing Institute for the Children of Military Men Fighting in the War of Resistance against Japan" was founded by the National Child Welfare Association in Shizi Mountain of Ciqikou of Chongqing. The Institute only recruited "children of military men who once fought in the War of Resistance against Japan". It was one of the Nursing Institutes of similar kinds that were established across China. Under the Chongqing Institute, there were General Affairs Section, Secretary Section, Accountant Section, Purchase & Maintenance Section, Educational Affairs Section, Nursing Section, Sanitation Section, Child Army Training Section, Living Affairs and Training Section, Training Service Section, Production Training Section, Infant Department and the other divisions.

重庆抗战军人子女教养院
Chongqing Nursing Institute for the Children of Military Men Fighting in the War of Resistance against Japan

丁肇中入读磁器口小学
Samuel Chao Chung Ting Enrolled in Ciqikou Elementary School

民国年间，磁器口掀起了创办新学的运动，教书先生范仲林将磁器口的著名道观宝善宫开辟为嘉陵小学，并任校长，嘉陵小学于1941年更名为"磁器口小学"。

抗战年间的1937年，丁肇中的父母从美国留学归来，在现今的重庆大学任教，家居磁器口。丁肇中在磁器口生活了8年，1942～1945年在嘉陵小学读书3年。据说，他小时候读书相当努力，尤其是数学题做得既快又好。1956年丁肇中到美国深造，1976年获诺贝尔物理学奖。在颁奖仪式上，他先用汉语做了讲演，开启了诺贝尔颁奖仪式上获奖者用两种语言进行两次演讲的先例。

During the years of the Republic of China, a movement of advocating new learning was initiated in Ciqikou. Teacher Fan Zhonglin transformed the Baoshan Taoist Temple into Jialing Elementary School. In 1941, the School was renamed as the Ciqikou Elementary School. In 1937, the one-year-old child Samuel Chao Chung Ting came to Chongqing with his parents who completed their study in the United States and returned home.

丁肇中入读磁器口小学
Samuel Chao Chung Ting Enrolled in Ciqikou Elementary School

华子良脱险
"Hua Ziliang" Escaping from White Residence and Zhazi Cave Prison

著名抗战小说《红岩》中有以鑫记杂货店为背景、描写华子良装疯卖傻传情报的故事。

华子良的原型人物，实为共产党人韩子栋。韩子栋是山东人，1909年生人，1933年加入共产党。1934年被捕，被关押14年之久。在监狱中他为了让看守对他放松警惕，便装疯卖傻，日子久了守卫见其又疯又傻便常常让它陪着去磁器口购货。1947年7月18日他陪看守到磁器口购货，趁看守打麻将之机穿过磁器口老街，渡过嘉陵江脱逃，经过45天的长途跋涉到达解放区。1992年这位英雄的老人在贵阳逝世，而华子良的故事，也永久地定格在了磁器口。

During the War of Resistance against Japan, there was the Family Xin's Grocery at No. 168 of Main Street of Ciqikou. In fact, this grocery was the secret underground liaison point in the east part of Sichuan. The Grocery was used to communicate information to the communists and the progressives in Zhazi Cave Prison or White Residence. The famous Novel Red Crag that depicts the War of Resistance against Japan features the story of Hua Ziliang pretending to be insane for communicating intelligence through the Family Xin's Grocery.

华子良脱险
"Hua Ziliang" Escaping from White Residence and Zhazi Cave Prison

荣强牙科诊所　Rongqiang Dental Clinic

郭沫若抗战时期居住在沙坪坝附近时，磁器口是其常来常往之地，古镇上的牙科医生江容强与其交好，曾为其治疗牙病，郭沫若为其题写了"容强牙科诊所"的匾，此匾仍存。

The first name of the dentist was Jiang. In according to the gossip, the grandfather of the dentist was the best friend of Guo Moruo. Therefore, Guo created this horizontal inscribed board as a gift.

荣强牙科诊所
Rongqiang Dental Clinic

徐悲鸿创作《巴人汲水图》
Xu Beihong Creating the *Water-Drawing Graph of People from Chongqing and Sichuan*

徐悲鸿（1895～1953），江苏宜兴人。中国现代画家、美术教育家。抗战期间曾在重庆居住，1938年绘制了《巴人汲水图》。该图高300厘米、宽62厘米，有舀水、让路、登高三个部分，描画了当年嘉陵江畔民众的生活景象。或许由于这幅画创作于战乱时期，对于《巴人汲水图》的绘画背景，徐悲鸿并没有留下更多的解释。

Xu Beihong (1895 ～ 1953), was from a native of Yixing, Jiangsu Province. He was a Chinese modern painter and educator of art. During the War of Resistance against Japanperiod of anti-Japanese War, Xu Beihong was livingresided in Chongqing. In 1938, to express the traditional scene of the Chongqing and Sichuan natives fetching water, Xuherepresented the traditional scene of the people from Chongqing and Sichuan drawing in the namecreated theof Graph of Water-Drawing People from Chongqing and Sichuan Water-Drawing Graph of People from Chongqing and Sichuanby thethrough the means integratinged approach of adopting both the Chinese techniques and the western techniques. The height and width of this Water-Drawing Graph of People from Chongqing and Sichuanis about 300 cm and 62 cm respectively. There are 3 parts of this painting, including namely, water-drawing, giving way and ascending high, thus. The Ggraph describing describes the life scenedaily life of the people living by the Jialingjia River of those years.

徐悲鸿创作《巴人汲水图》
Xu Beihong Creating the *Water-Drawing Graph of People from Chongqing and Sichuan*

张书旂创作《百鸽图》
Zhang Shuqi Creating the *White Pigeons Painting*

　　张书旂（1900～1957），浙江浦江人，曾任南京中央大学教授，工于中国画。抗战期间他住在重庆沙坪坝一带，1938年在此创作了《白鸽图》。1941年，这幅画作被当作礼物送给了当时的美国总统罗斯福，成为悬挂在美国白宫的第一幅中国画。

　　张书旂绘制《百鸽图》时，正值日军轰炸机不时在重庆上空狂轰滥炸的时候，他不惧危险，专程到磁器口买来家鸽，并把鸽子饲养在家中，整日专心观察鸽子，对鸽子的习性烂熟于心。《百鸽图》从构思到动笔到完成，仅仅用了三周的时间，100只栩栩如生的鸽子便跃然纸上。

Zhang Shuqi (1900 ～ 1957), a native of from Pujiang, Zhejiang Province, was once a professor of National Central University in Nanjing. He was good at Chinese drawing and was titled as one of "the Three Outstanding Men of Nanjing" along with Xu Beihong and Luzigu. During the War of Resistance against Japanperiod of anti-Japanese War, he lived in Shapingba of Chongqing. During his stay, where he created Drawing of White Pigeons in 1938, and he taking took the pigeons which representsthat wereas a symbol of peace to express Chinese people's desire for peace. In 1941, Drawing of White Pigeons was presented to Roosevelt, the President of the United States, to urge the United States to join in international anti-Fascist War and join the force movement of establishing the new order for international peace.

张书旂创作《百鸽图》
Zhang Shuqi Creating the *White Pigeons Painting*

七七电影院　July 7th Cinema

　　磁器口正街 80 号，现为磁器口古镇民俗博物馆所在。其前身曾是重庆最早的乡村电影院。

　　1939 年 7 月，重庆的电影片商夏云湖等人在磁器口主持开办了重庆第一个乡村电影院"七七电影院"，当年这里是宣传抗战和进行社会教育的地方，上演的影片内容都和抗战和教育有关。电影院还组织编排、上演过一些进步戏剧。比如，郭沫若的《棠棣之花》、曹禺的《雷雨》《日出》等戏剧就曾在这里演出过。很多文化名人，比如徐悲鸿、沈钧儒等都是这里的常客。

In July 1939, movie producer Xia Yunhu and other colleagues founded the "July 7th Cinema". In those years, this cinema was a place to promote publicity work on the War of Resistance against Japan and to conduct social education programs. All the movies played in this cinema were related to the War of Resistance against Japan and education. Moreover, some advanced dramas were organized and performed in the cinema. For instance, Flower of Shadbush by Guo Moruo, Thunderstorm by Cao Yu, Sunrise and so on were once performed in this cinema. Many cultural figures once went to this cinema to enjoy the drama. For instance, Xu Beihong, Shen Junru and other celebrities were the frequent callers of the cinema.

七七电影院
July 7th Cinema

自然地理与建筑

Geography & Architecture

磁器口古镇背靠歌乐山,面临嘉陵江(流经磁器口段2251米),被"两溪"之清水溪、凤凰溪环绕,"三山"之金碧山、马鞍山、凤凰山环抱。

　　古镇有传统街巷9条、不可移动文物12处、历史建筑4处、登录文物点2处、历史要素9处、入名录古树6棵。

Embraced by verdant hills and clean waters, Ciqikou is not far from the Jialing River that facilitates the town's water transport, and once served as the northern gateway to the ancient Chongqing City. The town was built in between 998 and 1003. Early in the Ming Dynasty (1368 ～ 1644 A.D.), the town already thrived as the commercial port which linked water and land transport, thus attracting numerous merchants and creating a unique culture. Historically, Ciqikou was known as the "Little Chongqing".

嘉陵江 Jialing River

嘉陵江是长江上游的支流，因流经陕西凤县东北的嘉陵谷而得名。干流流经陕西、甘肃、四川、重庆，在重庆朝天门汇入长江。全长 1345 千米，流域面积 16 万平方千米。磁器口嘉陵江段江宽岸阔、水波平静，是磁器口成为天然良港的优良条件。

The Jialing River is a branch at the upper stream of the Yangtze River. It is named so because it flows through the Jialing Valley northeast to the Xifeng County of Shaanxi Province. The River's main stream flows through Shaanxi Province, Gansu Province, Sichuan Province and Chongqing City, and affluxes into Yangtze River at Chaotianmen of Chongqing City. The main branches include: the Badu, Xihan, Bailong, Qujiang and Fujiang Rivers and etc.

嘉陵江
Jialing River

凤凰山　Phoenix Mountain

　　磁器口古镇的地貌被称作"一江两溪三山四街",凤凰山便是三山之一。凤凰山高耸于磁器口南端,海拔262米,是该地区最高峰。呈南北走向,山形酷似凤凰,方圆2华里,山上建有凤凰庙。抗战时期,教育部美术教育委员会曾迁设山上。1950年,附近工厂职工依山建房,农民在山上开荒种菜。今凤凰山绿树掩映,房舍点缀隐于其中。

Among the three mountains in the ancient town of Ciqikou, and the Phoenix Mountain is only one, on which people could have the full view of Ciqikou. Apart from being known as the location of the Phoenix Temple, the mountain was also a place gathering artists during the War of Resistance against Japan.

凤凰山
Phoenix Mountain

金碧山　Jinbi Mountain

金碧山，坐落在重庆特殊钢厂南面，金碧街正北之辖区境内。海拔240.1米，是磁器口地区的第二制高点。为当年的巴渝一景"金碧流香"。

古人有这样的描述："巴山顶名金碧山，左岩上有金碧台"，"巴山之顶名金碧山，即县学后山之祖峰也。府署左岩上有金碧台，明郡守张希召于台上建金碧山堂。俯瞰江城，饮虹览翠，每轻风徐过，馥馥然袭袂香流，寻之并无花木，岂心清闻妙香耶？""妙香吹不断，台踞石城脊。山外有夕阳，璀璨金与碧"。

The Jinbi Mountain is near the present Chang'an Temple (Cableway Station over the Yangtze River) The ancient people have such description of the mountain: "the peak of the Bashan Ridge is named as the Jinbi Mountain, and there is the Jinbi Stand on the left rock." "The name of the Bashan Mountain's peak is Jinbi, which is a major peak behind the county school. Zhang Xizhao, the governor of shire of the Ming Dynasty constructed the Jinbi Mountain Hall at the Jinbi Stand. Overlooking the town which named rivertown, climbers can enjoy tea and the green scenery, bathe in breeze and get indulged in the fragrance. However, there is no flower or wood behind such fragrance, and this feeling comes from a peaceful mind." "With fragrance all over in the atmosphere, the Jinbi Stand sits at the ridge and the sun sets beyond the mountain, shining the vivid golden and green colors." This was the major scenery of ChongQing which was known as "Fragrance Flowing in the Golden and Green Colors".

金碧山

Jinbi Mountain

马鞍山 Ma'an Mountain

马鞍山，西依歌乐山，东临嘉陵江，山形酷似马鞍。自童家桥东北部延伸至磁器口境内，横贯辖区中部，海拔234.6米，终止于嘉陵江边。

此山高居古镇中心，凤凰山、金碧山两山蹲其左右，登顶极目揽尽古镇山色。清代巴县知县王尔鉴曾有诗句赞曰：龙隐之山高以蠡，云树为衣石为骨。一峰峭削凿江波，两腋潆洄带溪谷。

With Gele Mountain in the west and Jialing River in the east, the Ma'an Mountain is named after its shape of a horse saddle. Originally, there was a white cliff (Baiya) on the mountain, so it is also known as the Baiya Mountain. According to legend, Emperor Jianwen of the Ming Dynasty once lived there in seclusion, so the mountain was renamed as the Longyin Mountain. Located in the center of the ancient town, this mountain has the Phoenix Mountain on the left and the Jinbi Mountain on the right. The scenery of the ancient town and mountains could be viewed at the peak of the Ma'an Mountain.

马鞍山
Ma'an Mountain

凤凰溪　Phoenix Creek

　　凤凰溪，发源于歌乐山的两条小溪。一条小溪溪名无考，源出歌乐山上高店子处，在杨家山北面与锅底函溪相汇。另一条小溪源于歌乐山东侧脚下的鸡冠山，在白公馆、渣滓洞公路东侧汇入几条小山沟溪水。干流全长7100米。凤凰溪自童家桥沿西南方向，蜿蜒曲折，至东北方向到老米市岩下入嘉陵江。

The Phoenix Creek is also known as the Jinbi Creek or Xiaojie Creek. The Creek originates from the Jingshi Water Bend southwest to the Yunding Temple of Geleshan Town. Winding and zigzagging southwestward along Tongjia Bridge, Phoenix Creek flows into Jialing River northeastward at Laomishiyan (which literally means the Rock of Ancient Rice Market).

凤凰溪
Phoenix Creek

清水溪　Qingshui Creek

清水溪，从歌乐山山洞村天灯杆蜿蜒而下，在磁器口古镇龙隐码头南侧汇入嘉陵江。干流全长约 19 千米，磁器口段长 1500 米。流域内共有山洞村、天池村等众多村庄。早年间，这里人们的生活和溪水息息相关，在溪边淘米洗衣、捉鱼虾、戏水玩耍。

The Qingshui Creek covers a drainage area of 35.54 km^2, and the overall length of the Creek's main stream is 19 km long. Coming deviously downward from Gele Mountain, Qingshui Creek flows into Jialing River in the ancient town of Ciqikou. Within the drainage area, there are 30 villages, including Shandong Village and Tianchi Village. In the early years, the residents washed clothes, played with water and caught fish and shrimps in the creek.

清水溪
Qingshui Creek

九石缸河滩　Nine Stone Jars Benchland

磁器口一带的嘉陵江畔，江边有宽大的河滩，江中有一条石梁子。石梁子上有一溜九个石包，远看就像是九个装水的大石缸。因此，石梁子得名"九石缸"。

河滩上曾出土过新石器时代的石器。1939年重庆中央大学的学者曾在河滩处发掘汉代崖墓群，墓壁上有"永寿四年"（公元158年）、"延熹五年"（公元162年）的题记，并出土陶俑、陶器若干。

相传九石缸为明末张献忠攻入重庆的"宝地"，传说张献忠占领重庆后，曾将重庆府库银悉数埋藏于九石缸河滩之中，所以至今仍有不少人到此寻宝。"石缸对石鼓，金银万万数，谁人解得开，买下重庆府"的民谣流传至今。

Located by the Jialing River in the center of the Jialing River, there are several narrow and long stone bulges. From the upper part to the lower part of the bulge, there are 9 stone enclaves in sequence. Looking from afar, the narrow and long stone bulges resemble 9 big stone water vats. Such bulges were thus named as 9-Stone Vat and had another name of 9-Stone Hillock. There have been numerous stories on the Stone Vat. According to some legends, the Stone Vat was the lucky land through which Zhang Xianzhong made his way into Chongqing.

九石缸河滩
Nine Stone Jars Benchland

古渡口　Ancient Ferry

　　位于嘉陵江边，形成于唐宋之间，繁荣于明清之际。明代文坛"前七子"诗人王廷相有"苍山冥冥落日尽，古渡渺渺行人稀"的诗句赞美这里。民国时达到极盛，有"白日里千人拱手，入夜来万盏明灯"之说。

　　民国十四年（1925年），国民政府专门设置了囤船，开通了磁器口至桂花园航线。

Located by the Jialing River, the Ferry was formed between the Tang and Song Dynasties, and thrived in the Ming and Qing Dynasties. Wang Tingxiang, one of the Former Seven Great Poets of the Ming Dynasty (1368 ～ 1644 A.D.) wrote the poem that depicted the "sun sets beyond the Cangshang Mountain, scarce passers-by walking in the ancient ferry". Before thriving during the period of the Republic of China. There was a legend on the Ferry that goes: "thousands of people cupping one hand in the other before their chests in daytime, and numerous lamps radiating in evening". In the 14th Year of the Republic of China (1925), the National Government set up the block ship in a special endeavor and opened the route from Ciqikou to Guihuayuan.

古渡口
Ancient Ferry

凤凰寺 Phoenix Temple

凤凰寺，位于磁器口对面的凤凰山上，据传因凤凰山形似凤凰而得名。始建于明（1368～1644）初期，至今已有600多年的历史。据史料记载，明中期和清嘉庆（1796～1820）年间有两次重建。

The Phoenix Temple is located at the Phoenix Mountain, which was named so because it in the similar shape to a phoenix. Built originally in the early Ming Dynasty (1368～1644), the Phoenix Temple has a history of more than 600 years. According to historical records, there were two times of reconstructions during the mid-term of the Ming Dynasty and the reign of Emperor Jiaqing (1796～1820) of the Qing Dynasty.

凤凰寺
Phoenix Temple

宝轮寺　Baolun Temple

建于明成化年间（1465～1487），占地面积近 400 平方米，是重庆市最负盛名的佛教名刹之一。传说建文帝朱允炆被其四叔燕王朱棣逼迫退位而辗转流落到磁器口避难时，曾在此隐居，遂又称龙隐寺。其大殿前檐下有一牌匾写着"大雄宝殿"，是由已故中国佛教协会主席、中国书法家协会名誉主席赵朴初题写。在清代康熙年间宝轮寺曾进行大修，使其规模远远超过明代。后来历经多次劫难，但大殿建筑和主佛释迦牟尼佛像得以保存。

The Baolun Temple is also known as the Longyin (Hidden Dragon) Temple. The Temple was constructed in early Tang Dynasty . It is located on the opposite side to the arcade of Ciqikou, As the legend reads that Emperor Jianwen once sought asylum in the Baolun Temple, the Temple was known as the "Longyin Temple" (a temple where a dragon, the symbol of a secluded emperor).

宝轮寺
Baolun Temple

宝轮寺·大雄宝殿
Great Buddha's Hall of Baolun Temple

　　宝轮寺大雄宝殿建筑面积约250平方米，为重檐歇山式建筑，斗拱木结构。采用一人不能合抱的马桑木做木柱穿逗支撑，未用一颗铁钉。更为神奇的是，大殿中那根双龙盘柱的基石一高一低，一边凸出地面尺许，一边凹下数寸，历经千年而不倾斜。殿内采光均匀，外面风雨不能入殿，殿内佛香烟尘却能排出殿外，设计独到，堪称绝妙。

Occupying an area of near 250 square meters, the wooden hall is supported only by pillars of coriariasinic, each one of which could not be encircled by a person. The structure is free of iron nails. Magically, one of footstones of two pillars engraved with dualdragon is somehow above the ground and the other is buried in the ground, and both of them have fallen down for a thousand years.

宝轮寺·大雄宝殿
Great Buddha's Hall of Baolun Temple

宝善宫　Baoshangong Taoist Temple

　　位于磁器口正街128号的一所古香古色的木建筑，此为磁器口历史上九宫十八庙中的道观宝善宫。在民国期间改为嘉陵小学，丁肇中先生曾就读于此。现该院改建为茶文化体验馆，系统展示茶、陶瓷与磁器口文化发展的历史轮廓。

　　宝善宫的一草一木、一砖一瓦都有鲜明的"金木水火土"五行之特色。为表达木建筑不受火灾之意，建筑的大门不在中国传统建筑中轴线上，而是偏向东南，面向嘉陵江，暗合"水火相克"。天井呈梯形，有16步梯坎，中有巨大的拜台。

The Baoshangong Temple is a well-known Taoist temple in the ancient town of Ciqikou. The town's buildings follow the Taoist concepts of Yin-Yang as well as the Five Elements of "Metal, Wood, Water, Fire and Earth". The main gate is not opened at the median line of temple's axis as the usual practice, but moved southeastward to face the Jialing River.

宝善宫
Baoshangong Taoist Temple

宝善宫·古井
Ancient Well in Baoshangong Taoist Temple

　　宝善宫庭院内天井开阔，中间的拜台专供善男信女上香跪拜、祈福求愿。拜台上有一口古井，相传井中水乃神水。祈福之人跪拜后须用井水净手，再到大殿叩头许愿，如此才会灵验。

The courtyard features a big ladder-shaped dooryard. In the dooryard, there is a worshipping stage, which is used by the devout men and women to offer incense to Buddha and kowtow for expressing their good wish. An ancient well could be found on the worshipping stage, and the water in this well is regarded as the divine water. According to legend, after the worshipping people complete their ceremony of kowtowing, they must wash their hands by water drawn from the well, and then go to the grand hall for kowtowing to express their good wish. Only in this way could their wishes be realized.

宝善宫 · 古井
Ancient Well in Baoshangong Taoist Temple

深水井　Shenshui Well (Deep Well)

　　位于磁器口磁正街110号院内。相传,该处原是一口枯井,明建文帝朱允炆避难逃到磁器口,藏于枯井中,饥渴难忍之时,突然间一股清泉从井底喷涌而出。建文帝饮后饥渴顿消,躲过一劫,为此建文帝称其为生水井。老百姓又称为僧水井,后经多年误传,人们就叫它深水井了。

　　此井水水质清澈甘甜,常年不枯。

The Shenshui Well is located in No. 110 Courtyard of the Cizheng Street. According to legend, the Well was a dried out well originally. Zhu Yunwen, Emperor Jianwen of the Ming Dynasty fled to Ciqikou and once hided in this dried out well. He was very thirsty, and almost fainted. All of a sudden, a clear spring spouted out of the bottom of the well, and the water was sweet and fresh. After drinking the water, the feeling of thirsty disappeared, and the Emperor was lifted out of his difficulties. Emperor Jianwen was very pleased and called this well as Shengshui Well (Water-Generating Well). Due to misinterpretations for many years, people called this Well as Shenshuijing (Deep Well).

深水井

Shenshui Well (Deep Well)

文昌宫古寨遗址
Historic Site of Wenchanggong Taoist Temple

　　磁器口一带有很多宗教场所，号称九宫十八庙。文昌宫位于金碧山东麓靠江一隅，系道教宫观，原有前后三进殿宇，四周以石质寨墙、寨门围合，据清乾隆《巴县志》记载为明成华年间（1465～1487）建成，现文昌宫殿宇已被拆毁，仅存寨门一座及少部分寨墙，寨门是券拱式石门，由15块截面呈楔形的石材垒砌而成。

　　当地民谣："歌乐灵音寺、龙隐凤凰台、渠涪文昌水、石马桂花香。"各地文昌宫供奉的都是主宰功名禄位的文昌帝君（文星、文曲星）。磁器口文昌宫与其他文昌宫不同处在于，它和明建文帝藏身磁器口的传说有着密切的关系。

The Wenchanggong is a Taoist Temple in the ancient town of Ciqikou. Nowadays, only a historic site, a cornerstone and a gate were left. Among the large number of religious places in the region of Ciqikou, the Wenchanggong Temple is the most popular one of its kind. This temple worships God of Wenchang, who governs human being's social status in feudal China and is also known as "Wenxing" or "Wenquxing" (Star of Wisdom).

文昌宫古寨遗址
Historic Site of Wenchanggong Taoist Temple

太平桥　Taiping Bridge

太平桥，始建于清代，由民众捐钱修建。为石平桥型。

Constructed originally in the Qing Dynasty, the flat Taiping Bridge of stones was financed by the public.

太平桥
Taiping Bridge

双龙桥 Shuanglong Bridge

双龙桥，位于金碧街与磁器口横街之间的金碧溪上。建于清代，为清末乡绅陈元煊集资所建。其桥为三孔券拱石桥，长28.7米、宽4.3米；拱跨7.6米，三拱大小相同。桥两侧各雕有两个龙头龙尾，意为镇压洪水。

The Shuanglong Bridge is located over the Jinbi Creek between the Jinbi Street and the Side Street of Ciqikou. The Bridge was built and financed during the late Qing Dynasty by the country gentleman Chen Yuanxuan. With the length of 28.7 m and width of 4.3 m, this bridge is an arch stone bridge with three holes. All the three arches are of the same size, and each arch has a span of 7.6 m. At both facades of the bridge, there are sculptures of two dragon heads and two dragon tails to suppress flood.

双龙桥
Shuanglong Bridge

仁寿桥 Renshou Bridge

仁寿桥，位于磁南街。建于清宣统二年（1910年），由磁器口考出去的两名武举人出资修建。单拱石桥，桥长36米、宽4米，拱跨5米。

紧挨这座古桥后人新修了一座三孔石桥。古桥头砌了一座砖墙，封死了上古桥的路，古桥上野草丛生，成了丧失功能架在河上的"模型"。

Built in 1910, the 2nd year during Emperor Xuantong reign of Qing Dynasty, Renshou Bridge is located in the Cinan Street. With the length of 36 m, width of 4 m, and arch span of 5 m, the Bridge is made of stones with a single arch. It was financed by two successful candidates of imperial Kongfu examination at provincial level from Ciqikou.

仁寿桥
Renshou Bridge

古旧民居
Architectural Complex of Folk Houses

　　磁器口古镇比较完好地保存着许多古老民居建筑。这些建筑见证了磁器口某一时期重大的历史事件，也反映了磁器口在某一时代独特的生产、生活状况和文化特征。虽经历百年之沧桑，但这些古旧民居仍会给今人另一番感受。

　　这些建筑曾均为风韵犹存、布局雅致的四合院。其特色为天井极小，屋檐水集向天井，由一枚铜钱形的地漏排出，暗合"肥水不流外人田"之意。例如，幸福街7号、21号、39号、55号民居，都是有物可看、有事可述的历史遗存。

Currently in the ancient town of Ciqikou, the architectural complex of folk houses has been well preserved. These houses all feature elegant layout, and are shaped as quadrangle courtyards with an everlasting appeal. The water flows down from eave and converges to the very small dooryard before being drained through a ground leakage in the shape of copper coin. Such design implies that "residents are able to keep the goodies within the family". This layout also reflects Ciqikou's unique characteristics of production, life and culture in a specific era in the history.

古旧民居
Architectural Complex of Folk Houses

古旧民居
Architectural Complex of Folk Houses

古旧民居
Architectural Complex of Folk Houses

青石老街　Bluestone Ancient Street

　　磁器口老街的石板路全由上好的青石铺就而成，习称青石老街。青石老街，最老者已有千年历史，真实记录了古镇的岁月沧桑。所以人们常说的"一条石板路，千年磁器口"，绝非妄言。

　　青石老街窄处仅两三米，宽处与街边房屋高度之比大体为 1∶1.5～1.8，暗合黄金定律。走在青石老街上，抬眼所见房屋，高低错落、极富韵味。

Bluestone Ancient Street is located in the Ancient Town of Ciqikou. The flagging of the ancient street of Ciqikou was laid by bluestone of superior quality, and the most ancient stones of the street has the history of more than 1000 years, genuinely recording the vicissitudes of the ancient town's history. Therefore, it is always said that "A slabstone road has witnessed a thousand years' history of Ciqikou". The narrow part of the ancient street of Ciqikou was only 2 to 3 meters, and the ratios between its width and the houses along the street coincide with the golden rule of construction, namely in the range between 1:1.5 to 1.8.

青石老街（磁横街部分）
Bluestone Ancient Street

青石老街（幸福街部分）
Bluestone Ancient Street

青石老街（磁正街部分）
Bluestone Ancient Street

高石坎　High Stone Ladder

　　高石坎，位于磁器口正街。拾级而上的石梯与依山而建的穿斗结构板壁房，既是磁器口古镇的标志性景观，也是巴渝山地民居建筑的典型代表。

The High Stone Ladder is located in Main Street of Ciqikou. In the High Stone Ladder, there are the ascending stone ladder steps, the wooden plate house with the through type plate wall structure. The Ladder constitutes the symbolic scenery of the ancient town of Ciqikou and is also the typical representative of the mountainous folk houses of Chongqing City and Sichuan Province.

高石坎
High Stone Ladder

磁正街　Ciqikou Main Street

　　磁正街，磁器口古镇的正街，位于古镇核心保护区内。平均宽约 5 米，最窄处约 3 米，最宽处约 8 米，由上好青石板铺成，全长约 640 米，两边多为传统店宅和工艺作坊，街宽与房屋高度比为 1:1.5～1.8 之间，暗合黄金定律，尺度宜人，自然和谐，保存完好，属于规划的核心保护区。是古镇的最主要街巷。街区内的古旧民居保存完好，磁器口古镇的历史遗址多分布于此。

Located in the core reserve area of the ancient town, the Ciqikou Main Street is the most critical street in the ancient town. Within the street, the houses have been well preserved, and the historic sites and stores spread primarily in the Ciqikou Main Street.

磁正街
Ciqikou Main Street

磁横街　Ciqikou Side Street

　　磁横街，磁器口古镇的横街，位于古镇核心保护区内，是古镇的主要街巷。平均街宽约 3 米，全长约 240 米。街区内古旧民居保存完好，磁器口古镇的重要寺庙宝轮寺即在此巷。

　　如今的磁横街汇聚了各式的酒吧、咖啡吧、书吧、茶社、创意工坊，已经成为磁器口景区标志性街区，是领略磁器口古镇历史文化和现代休闲文化形态的最佳场所。

Located in the core reserve area of the ancient town, Ciqikou Side Street constitutes a major street. The Side Street has an average width of about 3 meters, and the full length of the Street is about 240 m. The houses have been preserved intact in the block. Baolun Temple, the critical temple of the ancient town, is located in this Street. Currently, the Side Street of Ciqikou has witnessed the flourishing of bars, cafes, book stores, tea houses, innovation workshop, and the Street has thus become the landmark block within the Ciqikou scenic area. The Street is also regarded as the best place to appreciate the historical culture and modern leisure cultural forms of the ancient town of Ciqikou.

磁横街

Ciqikou Side Street

翰林院　Hanlin Academy

　　翰林院，位于磁器口古镇小巷内。原为鲤鱼石学舍，清末在此办学授课，学生中曾有3人考中为举人。所以，翰林院是当时读书人向往之地。

　　目前老建筑中的中院尚存，内庭有一座小拜月台，是当年主人举行家庭祭祀的地方。现在这里已改建为"翰林茶园"。

The Hanlin Academy of Ciqikou was Carp Stone School originally. In the late years of Qing Dynasty, the Academy was operated in the current area for conducting lectures, and three successful candidates in the imperial examinations at the provincial level came from this Academy. Therefore, the Hanlin Academy was the desirable place for students at that time. Currently, the house of academy has been well preserved in the middle courtyard. Within the inner courtyard, there is a small moon-worshipping stage where the master held family worship ceremony.

翰林院
Hanlin Academy

鑫记杂货店　Grocery Store of The Xin's

　　磁器口正街168号，抗战期间这里曾开有一个鑫记杂货店，该小店当时实为中共沙磁区委地下联络点。小店面阔一间3.3米，进深一间5.3米，面积17.49平方米。目前，其外墙镶嵌有用黑色大理石制作的中英文"原中共沙磁区委地下联络点"标牌。室内按当年的原貌布置，并增设了韩子栋生平事迹展览。韩子栋为《红岩》小说中"疯老头"华子良的原型，店内陈设了韩子栋各个阶段的传奇经历。

The Xins' Grocery was opened at No. 168 of Main Street of Ciqikou during the War of Resistance against Japan. This grocery was actually the secret underground contact point of the CPC Shaci District Committee, with the width of 3.3 meters, the depth of 5.3 meters and the area of 17.40 square meters. At present, a black marble is inlaid the *Original Underground Contact Point of the CPC Shaci District Committee* in Chinese and English on the exterior wall. The interior is arranged according to the original appearance of that year, and an exhibition of the life stories of Han Zidong was added. Han Zidong is the prototype of Hua Ziliang, the *mad old man in the novel Red Creg*. The grocery exhibits the legendary experience of various stages of Han Zidong.

鑫记杂货店
Grocery Store of The Xin's

钟家院　The Zhong's Courtyard

　　钟家院，建成于 1890 年前后，主人是在磁器口长大的钟云亭老先生。整个院子既有北方院落的中轴线格局，又大量运用了南方建筑的装饰手法。庭院现仅存前院、厢房、厅房和厨房等房屋 20 余间，前厅、正厅等建筑的主体木结构保留完整。近年作为展示清代民俗生活的场所开放。

Family Zhong's Courtyard was built at about1890. Its master was the senior gentleman ZhongYunting, who grew up in Ciqikou. This courtyard has integrated the lasting appeal of quadrangle courtyards in North China and the delicacy and elegance of folk houses in South China. In the courtyard, there are the antique beds of the Ming and Qing Dynasties, tables of blooming flowers and full moon and other cultural antiques available for exhibition. Therefore, the courtyard is a critical place representing the folk houses of the Qing Dynasty.

钟家院
The Zhong's Courtyard

童家院子　The Tong's Courtyard

童家院子，位于磁器口汲水巷 1 号，清代民居院落。

Located at No.1, Jishui Alley, Ciqikou, Family Tong's Courtyard is one of the folk houses of the Qing Dynasty.

童家院子
The Tong's Courtyard

江防碉堡
Jiangfang Pillbox (the Pillbox along Yangtze River)

江防碉堡，位于磁器口文昌寨北侧，架高来石刻之上。碉楼建于20世纪20年代，为当时的重庆电力钢厂为保卫厂区安全所建。碉堡为石砼结构，三层，外墙使用石块垒砌，顶部为钢筋混凝土结构平顶。碉堡所在位置居高临下，面向江心，可控制嘉陵江广大水域。

画家吴作人于抗战时期曾在此居住，并在此创作了《抗战三部曲》《重庆大轰炸》等重要作品。

The Jiangfang Pillbox was the former dwelling of Wu Zuoren when he taught in National Central University in Chongqing during the War of Resistance against Japan. In June 1940, the original residence of Wu Zuoren was bombed by Japanese aircrafts. With no other choice, Wu moved to an abandoned pillbox on the Phoenix Mountain of Ciqikou and lived there in struggle. In this dwelling, he created the Trilogy of the War of Resistance against Japan, the Bombing of Chongqing and other masterpieces.

江防碉堡
Jiangfang Pillbox (the Pillbox along Yangtze River)

架高来石刻

Stone Carving of "*Jia Gao Lai*" (three Chinese Characters to warn boats that the water is deep and flow is rapid ahead)

"架高来",摩崖题刻,位于铧拖嘴河滩旁的悬崖上,现存两幅。

北侧一幅为阴刻楷书"架高来"三字,以警示来往船只。字大小约1米,为清光绪年间乡人吴筱菘所书。

南侧一幅为一首警世诗,行书阴刻,题刻宽2.5米、高1.25米,字大小15厘米。内容为:"划拖嘴上浪飞埃,过此渐世免战牌。一载惊魂都付与,三言警语架高来。贪生转舵多为鬼,拼死向崖必退灾。信有观音能镇水,千年古道雾重开。"

The stone carving of "*Jia Gao Lai*" is on the rock wall beside the Wenchang Taoist Temple. There are two stone carvings on north side and south side respectively. On north side, the stone carving is three incised Chinese characters in regular script "Jia Gao Lai" (which literally means three Chinese Characters to warn boats that the water is deep and flow is rapid ahead), and each of these characters has a diameter of about 1m. On south side, the stone carving is cautionary poem, which is incised in semi-cursive script.

架高来石刻

Stone Carving of "*Jia Gao Lai*" (three Chinese Characters to warn boats that the water is deep and flow is rapid ahead)

小重庆碑   Little Chongqing Stele

　　小重庆碑，立于磁器口古镇的丁字口。该碑系当年的国民党主席林森的题刻，他游览磁器口，见其繁荣有感而发所作。现碑为 2000 年重刻。原碑已毁。

The Stele is located at the T-junction of the ancient town. The inscription on the stele was written by Lin Sen. He visited Ciqikou and wrote the script as he was inspired by the prosperity of Ciqikou. The original stele had been destroyed, and the current stele was re-engraved in 2000.

小重庆碑
Little Chongqing Stele

抗日阵亡将士纪念碑
Cenotaph for Sacrificed Officers and Soldiers in the War of Resistance against Japan

　　1937 年七七事变后，日军大规模侵略中国。时任国民党副总裁的汪精卫、陈璧君夫妇叛国投敌，一时引起全国公愤。1940 年在爱国将领冯玉祥的主持下，向社会各界募捐在磁器口的新街口修建了抗日阵亡将士纪念碑，同时在纪念碑前放置了青石雕汪精卫夫妇双手反缚、俯首长跪的雕塑。

　　现存生铁铸汪逆跪像为 2002 年重新制作。

In 1940, General Feng Yuxiang took charge of the construction of this cenotaph, and Professor Wang Yilin served as the designer and creator. Due to financial constraint, the original sculpture of Wang Jingwei Kneeling Down was engraved out of bluestone. It was buried deeply underground during construction of road in the 1950s. The current sculpture of Wang Jingwei, which was remade in 2002, is casted with iron.

抗日阵亡将士纪念碑
Cenotaph for Sacrificed Officers and Soldiers in the War of Resistance against Japan

四川省立教育学院旧址
Site of Sichuan Provincial Education College

　　两栋近代建筑，位于磁器口金沙正街，现重庆市第二十八中学旧址内。建筑皆坐南朝北，砖木结构混合式风格。东侧一栋占地面积432平方米，西侧一栋占地面积390平方米。均保存完好，具有一定的历史与文物价值。

　　1933年7月，四川省政府在四川中心农事试验场的地域上正式成立四川乡村建设学院，招收本科学生100余人。1936年四川乡村建设学院改名为四川省立教育学院。1937年抗战全面爆发，该校大量接纳西迁来渝的师生，并成为"重庆沙坪文化区自治委员会"发起单位和主要成员之一。

The College is located in the current area of 28th Middle School of Chongqing, Jinsha Main Street, At present, two modern buildings have been preserved in this site. Facing to north, both buildings are masonry and wood structure. The College's predecessor was the Sichuan Rural Construction College built in July 1933. When the War of Resistance against Japan broke out, the College received a large number of teachers and students who migrated westward to Chongqing.

四川省立教育学院旧址
Site of Sichuan Provincial Education College

井中天茶坊

Jingzhongtian (which literally means Sky in the Well) Tea House

　　位于磁器口古镇的幸福街。幸福街 55 号民居曾作为法国教会医院的院址，现作为茶坊使用。

In the ancient town of Ciqikou, there are the folk house clusters which have been preserved well. Happiness Street is one of the buildings which are preserved intact. The building at No. 55 of Happiness Street is the first ancient building well preserved in this street. The buildings had been the historical site of French Church Hospital and became Jingzhongtian Tea House subsequently.

井中天茶坊
Jingzhongtian (which literally means Sky in the Well) Tea House

聚森茂酱园　Jusenmao Sauce and Pickles Shop

　　清光绪十八年（1892年）张杰三继承父业，在磁器口"官盐店"的旧址上开办了作坊式酱园，取名"聚森茂酱园"，是重庆近代酿造行业中历史最悠久、影响最深远的老字号酱园。"聚森茂"现位于磁器口金蓉正街，建筑保存了传统古建筑风格，门店有自己生产的所有产品。

Located at Jinrong Main Street, "Jusenmao Sauce and Pickles Shop" has been the time-honored brand which has the longest history and the most profound influence in the brewing industry of Chongqing in modern times. This sauce and pickles shop was founded by Zhang Zhenggang in Duzibei Street (current Caiyuanba) of Chongqing City in 1885, the 11th year during Emperor Guangxu's reign. In the 18th Year of Emperor Guangxu (1892), his son Zhang Jiesan bought the "Official Salt Store" in Ciqikou which had been closed out to open a workshop style sauce and pickles shop, and named this shop as Jusenmao Sauce and Pickles Shop.

聚森茂酱园
Jusenmao Sauce and Pickles Shop

风土人情

Local Customs and Practices

来吧，把磁器口的小吃吃个遍，陈麻花、红油火锅、烩千张、凉粉、鸡杂、黄糕粑、脆辣椒、臭豆腐……

来吧，到磁器口坐坐大红花轿、听听金钱板和莲花闹，或者亲手泡一碗坝坝茶……

磁器口，距离闹市不远，距离江水青山很近很近……

Come and try the fried Dough Twist of Family Chen, Hot Pot of Red Soup and Yellow Rice Cake. Stinky tofu in Ciqikou…

Come and sit in the red sedan chair, listen Jinqian Plate and lianhuanao Opera in Ciqikou…

Ciqikou, not far from downtown area. But close to green mountains and rivers…

揽载帮 好吃船
Offering Food and Beverage for Boatmen

当年,嘉陵江上游的沱江、保宁河、渠江等支流的各种货船载着上游各地的土特产,直航重庆千厮门和临江门,统称为"小河揽载船"。磁器口是揽载船的中转码头,船工们经过长途跋涉,到达磁器口的时候正又累又饿、饥肠辘辘。他们见到岸边一只只小船里尽是物美价廉的磁器口小吃,如油炸锅魁、椒盐花生、五香豆腐干、沙炒葫豆和凉粉凉面等,便大快朵颐起来,旅途劳累也顿然消失。这就是当年嘉陵江上远近闻名的"磁器口码头的好吃船"。

In those years, the transport boat had large carrying capacity and low transport fee, whereas the boatmen were burdened by heavy labor and lived a hard life. The boat owner merely provided them with dried rice and pickles, and pork was only provided once every two weeks. The boatmen were exposed to wind and sun as years passed by. Ciqikou was the transiting port for carrier boats. After the hard-long journey, boatmen were tired and hungry when they arrived at Ciqikou. After those boatmen and the passengers departed from the upper reach and arrived at the Linjiang Gate, they had a meal and enjoyed liquor to satiety, then they had a rest for a while before the carrier boat set out again.

揽载帮 好吃船
Offering Food and Beverage for Boatmen

庙会　Temple Fair

庙会，是中国民间的宗教及岁时风俗，也是中国集市贸易形式之一。磁器口的庙会有着悠久的历史，如果追溯它的历史，可能要和磁器口的起源有很大的关系了。过去，每逢农历初一、十五，以及释迦牟尼出生日、观音菩萨生日、春节、放生日等，磁器口周边甚至更远地方的人们，都会到磁器口来赶庙会，烧香拜佛、求愿还愿，购买生活用品、品尝美食。

Previously, when people celebrated every beginning and the 15th of every lunar month, birth date of Sakyamuni, birth date of the Goddess of Mercy, spring festival, date of freeing captive animals and so on, the people who lived in the vicinity of Ciqikou and even those who came from more distant places would go to Ciqikou to attend the temple fair. In the temple, they would burn incense and worship the gods, seek help from gods and redeem a vow to gods, and they would purchase living goods and taste delicious food. Nowadays, the Ciqikou Temple Fair has more abundant activities featuring more cultural characteristics.

Generally speaking, the Ciqikou Temple Fair starts from December 24th of lunar year and ends at January 15th of lunar year, namely, the Lantern Festival.

庙会
Temple Fair

舞龙　Playing the Dragon

　　曾经每年的春节，从年三十开始一直到正月十五，磁器口都有舞龙灯的活动。每逢春节前，当地玩龙艺人用竹篾扎好火龙骨架，外面糊以皮纸或纱布，再浆上米汤，待干后画上龙甲并涂好油彩。龙身视表演规模的大小而定，一般以节为称，多用单数，舞龙时一人一节。

The "dragon dancing" activity was known in Ciqikou. Generally speaking, the "Dragon" was made from Bamboo, the very common local products. People used bamboo to weave the framework of the head, body and tail of the dragon. Then, people used the dragon scale cloth which is made of fabric to wrap over the framework of dragon. When the fire dragon dance is performed, the players wore colorful clothes, trousers, headband and flower shoes. One performer lifted the silk ball to tantalize the dragon, and the other player held each section of dragon to follow the silk ball. With the accompaniment of drum music, the dragon dance performers leveraged various movements such as passing through, writhing, jumping and rolling to express the spirit and charm of dragon.

舞龙
Playing the Dragon

坝坝茶　Baba Tea

云贵高原是个山脉连绵的地方，山间的那些小平地被人们称为"坝子"。坝坝茶是生活在这些坝子上的人们的一种生活习惯。

很早很早以前，老重庆人就有喝茶的习惯，因为天气炎热，人们还喜欢在露天喝茶。人们会在"坝子"的大树下，支起矮桌子和竹椅，用大长嘴的铜茶壶泡上盖碗茶，一边喝茶一边摆龙门阵，有的茶馆还有唱川剧的，优哉游哉。慢慢地，这种生活习惯，就被叫作"坝坝茶"了。

The Yunnan-Guizhou Plateau is a mountainous place, and the small flat ground is called by locals as "Bazi". Drinking Baba Tea has been a kind of life style for people living in these flat grounds.

Long time ago, the old natives of Chongqing had the habit of drinking tea. Due to the hot weather, local people also preferred drinking tea in open air. People would set up the low desk and bamboo chair under the big tree on the flat ground, and used the bronze teapot with long nozzle to make covered bowl tea. They drank tea and chatted with each other. In some of the teahouses, Sichuan Opera could be performed. Gradually, this kind of life habit is referred to as drinking the Baba Tea.

坝坝茶
Baba Tea

金钱板
Jinqian Plate (Small Rhythm Instrument made of Bamboo Plate with Copper Coin inlaid at the Upper End of the Bamboo Plate)

　　金钱板又叫金剑板、三才板,由演唱者手持竹子片互相敲打而得名,是主要流行于四川的一种曲艺演唱。传统书目有《三国》《水浒》《游江南》等"长条书";还有取材于民间寓言、故事、笑话的"诗头子"。武松赶会、闹庙、打店的三段故事被称为"买米书",当年最吸引观众。

　　金钱板由一人表演,边唱边说边打竹片。唱词通俗易懂,为七字句或十字句,每句字数不限,段末一句略有拖腔。演唱者两手分别持上端嵌有铜制钱的楠竹片,两手上的楠竹片互相敲击,从而打出不同的节奏、音响,据说可以敲打出风、云、雷、雨等九种声响。

Jinqian Plate is performed solo. While the performer is singing, he narrates the story and plays the bamboo plate simultaneously. The lyrics is usually popular and easy to understand, and is composed of sentence with 7 or 10 characters with no limited number of characters for sentences. At the end of each aria, there is a lasting tune. The performer holds the bamboo plates with copper coin inlaid by two hands, and the bamboo plates clashes each other to sound different rhythms and voices. Someone says that Jinqianban could sound 9 different voices of wind, cloud, thunder, rain and the others.

金钱板
Jinqian Plate (Small Rhythm Instrument made of Bamboo Plate with Copper Coin inlaid at the Upper End of the Bamboo Plate)

莲花闹

Lianhuanao Opera (a Popular Folk Art Form which literally means the Lotus Noise)

莲花闹是一种使用方言，用竹板打节拍，边说边唱的民间曲艺。莲花闹在磁器口也曾很流行。有一位名康森棣的老人自小住在磁器口，20世纪80年代退休后，他编写了不少"莲花闹"的新唱词。下录一首康森棣老先生关于磁器口的莲花闹词：

老街一条石板路，千年古镇情悠悠。
白崖千年兴闹市，建文龙隐水码头。
江氏兄弟开磁厂，张家父子造酱油。
孙家一门三举子，黄段二人做翰林。
冯大将军逆汪像，华子良脱逃在这头。
肇中获得诺贝尔，世界华人扬眉头。
政府保护磁器口，古镇人民争上游。

Lianhuanao Opera was a kind of folk-art form which was very popular in many places of China. Most of such operas were performed in local accents of different places. The performers used the bamboo plates to play rhythm, sing and narrate stories. For long time, the performers have been beggars.

Lianhuanao Opera was once very popular in Ciqikou. An old man with the name of Kang Sendi has lived in Ciqikou since he was a child. After retiring, he collected many historical materials of the ancient town of Ciqikou to compose new lyrics of Lianhuanao Opera, which featured Ciqikou's historical legends, cultural anecdotes, new living styles and trends of the times. Mr. Kang performed those new lyrics on street, at port and in teahouse for free.

莲花闹
Lianhuanao Opera (a Popular Folk Art Form which literally means the Lotus Noise)

花轿迎亲
Welcoming Bride by Bridal Sedan Chair

轿子原名"舆",是一种人工抬着前行的交通工具。相传春秋时期中国人就已经使用轿子了。轿子运用到娶亲上,最早见于宋代,后来才渐渐成为民俗。待嫁的新娘乘坐新郎家派来的大红花轿到婆家,是旧时婚姻仪式中的重要环节。用来娶亲的轿子,名花轿、喜轿,用红色来显示喜庆吉利,故俗称大红花轿。

古代的花轿,因各地的习俗、主人的贫富而有不同。普通人娶亲用的一般是二人抬的花轿,家境富贵之户常用四人抬的大花轿。罩轿子的帷子用大红色的彩绸,并绣有富贵花卉、丹凤朝阳和百子图等吉祥图案。到清朝末年,上海、北京等大城市,花轿逐渐被取代。

Sedan is a manual transportation means which is lifted by people. According to legends, as early as in Spring and Autumn Period, Chinese people started to use sedan. The earliest record of the use of a sedan to welcome a bride was found in Song Dynasty, and subsequently, such practice had gradually become the folk custom. The bride to be married in a great flower sedan sent by bridegroom went to bridegroom's family, which was a critical link during the wedding ceremony. The sedan used for taking bride is named as flower sedan, or bridal sedan. To express happiness and luck, the sedan is fabricated in red, and therefore it is commonly known as the great red flower sedan.

The flower sedans in ancient times varied from each other due to the difference of customs in different places as well as the varying wealth of the bridegroom's families. Generally speaking, common people used the flower sedan carried by two people to take bride, and the wealthy family used the flower sedan carried by four people.

花轿迎亲
Welcoming Bride by Bridal Sedan Chair

椒盐花生
Peanut Mixed with Spicy Salt

旧时，磁器口码头上常有盐船停靠，盐包在搬运时食盐撒落一地。在码头上找生活的小商贩们，会把散落于地的"盐灰"扫集起来，用来煮花生，做成下酒菜。逐渐，椒盐花生越做越讲究，不仅要用上等的花生，还要加入花椒、八角、三奈、小茴、桂皮等香料，更要用"聚森茂酱油"煮透。煮熟的花生，晾干水汽后用文火炕干。民国年间，磁器口的椒盐花生产量很大，花生炒房一家挨着一家，成为当年磁器口一景。

如今，磁器口的"椒盐花生"已经进入重庆著名小吃的行列。

Peanut mixed with spicy salt is a home dish popular all over China. The main ingredient is peanut, and the supplemental ingredients include fennel, cinnamon, Sichuan pepper and salt. The dish in Ciqikou has special flavors and is both crisp and tasty, thus becoming a well-known snack in Chongqing.

The peanut mixed with spicy salt of Ciqikou had became famous in the eastern part of Sichuan even prior to the War of Resistance against Japan. In the old days, there were salt boats docking at the port of Ciqikou, and salt was scattered on ground when the salt package was transported along the route.

The peddlers who sought to live on port would gather the scattered "salt dust", and boiled the peanut as the snacks for liquor, which was very popular among people.

椒盐花生
Peanut Mixed with Spicy Salt

毛血旺
Maoxuewang (Chongqing Style Boiled Blood Curd)

鸭血、猪血，民间称为血旺。毛血旺，也叫冒血旺，是渝菜江湖传统菜肴中非常著名的一道烫煮菜，成菜汤汁红亮、麻辣鲜香。

这道菜是将生血旺、毛肚、肥肠、各种青菜现烫现煮现吃。"毛"在重庆方言里有"粗犷"的意思，吃毛血旺是有讲究的，盆内的红油要透亮，不浑不浊。一般先吃肉类后吃豆腐、蔬菜。

现在，磁器口有相当多家的餐馆有"毛血旺"这道菜，各家有各家的特点。

Maoxuewang, which is known as the Chongqing style boiled blood curd, is a very famous scalded and boiled dish in Chongqing's traditional folk cuisine. Integrated with the full spectrum of four flavors, namely, the spicy, the hot, the fresh and the fragrant flavors, the soup of the finished dish is red and bright. Duck blood and pig blood have been commonly known as Xuewang. As for this dish, people scald and boil the fresh xuewang, cattle stomach, pig's intestines and various vegetables for a meal on the site.

Currently, there are many restaurants specialized in the dish of "Maoxuewang", and each has its own style of cuisine.

毛血旺
Maoxuewang (Chongqing Style Boiled Blood Curd)

红汤火锅　　Hot Pot of Red Soup

相传，清朝雍正年间，一位巡按途经磁器口，他突然嗅到一股诱人的香味，便立刻派人去寻找。殊不知，那香味来自灯笼桥下的几个叫花子破砂锅里的残羹剩饭。跟班的不敢如实禀报，而磁器口的厨师是个聪明人，他找来烧炭的小火炉，炉上支起一小砂锅，熬好骨头汤，调好麻辣卤汁，将切好的肉片、肝尖腰花片等，分装八个盘子随火锅送上。那巡按见到红的火、沸的红汤，立刻口水直流。问厨师这是道什么菜，厨师急中生智顺口答道："红汤火锅"。从此，红汤火锅流传开来。

红汤火锅发祥地就在磁器口，不过是不是在灯笼桥下，那可就不好说了。

Hot Pot of Red Soup is the traditional famous dish in Sichaun Province and Chongqing City. The dish is spicy, salt, fresh and of heavy flavor. The earliest hot pot in Ciqikou shared similar characteristics with the steam-boiler pole by the river of Nanjimen section. There was an earthen stove at one side of the pole, and a tinplate basin with grids in it on the stove. Within the basin, there was the boiled marinade which was spicy and hot. Each diner scalded the sliced beef offal and vegetables contained in dish platein each grid. After completion of their meals, the diners paid in accordance with the number of empty plates.

红汤火锅
Hot Pot of Red Soup

黄粑糕制作技艺
Manufacturing Workmanship of Yellow Rice Cake

黄糕粑，由糯米做成的，用竹笋壳、玉米皮包裹。金黄、润甜、滋润，营养丰富。

人们先要把糯米用清水浸泡半天，然后蒸成糯米饭，在凉了的糯米饭里拌上适量的红糖，还要把磨好的豆渣掺进去并拌匀。揉匀的糯米团用手捏成想要的大小，然后再包上洗净的竹笋壳、玉米皮。把做好的糯米团摆在甑子里，每摆上一层糯米团要铺上一层稻草，就这样一层层地将甑子摆满，然后盖上甑盖。蒸黄粑糕时，先用大火蒸三四个小时，然后文火蒸七八个小时。中途不能熄火，火也不能忽大忽小。

Yellow rice cake is made of sticky rice and is wrapped by skin of bamboo shots and corn bran. First, people immerse the sticky rice in clean water for half a day, and then steam the rice into glutinous rice. After the rice is cooled, it is mixed with a moderate amount of red sugar before being mixed with bean dregs and mix thoroughly. Subsequently, the sticky rice balls are rolled to the desirable size, and are then wrapped with the clean skin of bamboo shots and corn bran. Next, the yellow rice cake is steamed by big fire for 3 or 4 hours, and then by small fire for 7 or 8 hours. The fire shall not be extinguished halfway, and the fire shall be stable. In this way, the yellow rice cake will become golden in color, sweet and moist in taste, and abundant in nutrition.

黄粑糕制作技艺
Manufacturing Workmanship of Yellow Rice Cake

陈麻花制作技艺
Manufacturing Workmanship of Fried Dough Twist of Family Chen

磁器口古镇上，到处都有卖麻花的店铺，而且很多招牌打的是"陈麻花"的旗号。这些店铺几乎都用前店后厂的传统方式在制作麻花、出售麻花。磁器口的麻花都是手工制作的，酥脆、香甜，被形容为"嚼着惊动十里人"。

在磁器口，做麻花的历史可以追溯到清代，清末"陈麻花"已经小有名气。近几十年，把麻花做得好吃、把生意做火的，是一位叫陈昌银的人，他发扬祖传秘方，不断推陈出新，他家的麻花口感酥软、口味独特，而且他做生意厚道、童叟无欺。陈麻花名声在外，连带磁器口的麻花生意也都好起来。"陈麻花"已经成了重庆特色小吃的代表，几乎成了磁器口的代名词。

In the ancient town of Ciqikou, there are many stores selling fried dough twist, and most of them are marketed in the name of "fried dough twist". All these stores follow the traditional way of front-store and back-workshop to manufacture and sell fried dough twist at the same time. The fried dough twist in Ciqikou is made manually.

In Ciqikou, the practice of making fried dough twist could date back to Qing Dynasty. By the end of Qing Dynasty, Fried Dough Twist of Family Chen just won its initial reputation. In recent decades, the one who has flourished the business of the fried dough twist is a man named Chen Changyin. He has carried forward the secret prescription handed down from ancestors and created new products. What's more, he has been known for his integrity and kindness in business. Fried Dough Twist of Family Chen has become the representative of Chongqing special snacks, which has become nearly the symbolof Ciqikou.

陈麻花制作技艺
Manufacturing Workmanship of Fried Dough Twist of Family Chen

聚森茂酱油制作技艺
Manufacturing Workmanship of Jusenmao Soy Sauce

"聚森茂"酿造厂是重庆鼎鼎有名的老字号,"聚森茂"三字意为聚集财宝就像森林一样繁茂。创始人张杰三在酱油生产上十分讲求质量信誉,所以生意奇特的好。后来,张杰三之子张广厚和其孙张载坤改良了酱油生产工艺,采用霉菌等微生物发酵的科学方法,缩短了配制时间,不仅降低了成本,还提高了产品质量。一时间,全国各地来此学习其酱油技术的络绎不绝,聚森茂酱油也更是名扬四方。

The old famous brand of Jusenmao Sauce and Pickle Store has been the one with the longest history and imposes the most profound influence in the brewing industry of Chongqing in modern times. According to records, the Store was founded by Zhang Zhenggang in the 11th year of Emperor Guangxu of Qing Dynasty (1885). About 7 or 8 years later, Zhang Zhenggang's son Zhang Jiesan founded the sauce and pickle workshop at the former site of "official salt store", and the products included soy sauce, bran vinegar and thick broad-bean sauce.

"Jusenmao" Store is an ambitious workshop. The Store would absorb any new technology to upgrade its own workmanship.

Currently, "Jusenmao" Store is located at Jinrong Main Street with buildings of the traditional style of architecture. In the Store, all of its products are exhibited for sale.

聚森茂酱油制作技艺
Manufacturing Workmanship of Jusenmao Soy Sauce

千张制作技艺
Manufaturing Workmanship of Qianzhang (Dried Pieces of Bean Curd)

千张，是磁器口当地生产的一种豆制品，其制作非常讲究。由千张烧成的"软烩千张"，是磁器口的一道名菜。

制作千张的主要原料是黄豆。黄豆先要用深水井的水浸泡，再在石磨上细磨成豆浆。用细白布将豆浆滤出浆汁，然后用文火熬煮。浆汁烧浓后，用细麻布铺一层滤一层，再铺再滤。等上一段时间，再把已经成型的豆皮一张一张的揭下来。千张由此得名。

Qianzhang (Dried Pieces of Bean Curd) is a kind of bean product made in Ciqikou. Its workmanship is very complicated. The softly-braised dried pieces of bean curd made of Qianzhang are a famous dish in Ciqikou.

The main ingredient of Qianzhang is soybean. First, the soybean is immersed in the water drawn from deep well before being grinded on the stone mill into soybean milk. Then the juice of soybean milk is filtered by fine white cloth, and then boiled on small fire. After the juice is condensed, the condensed juice is filtered and paved with fine linen cloth alternately layer by layer. After a while, the skin of bean curd which has been molded one by one is uncovered, and this is how Qianzhang (which literally means a thousand pieces) has earned its name.

千张制作技艺
Manufacturing Workmanship of Qianzhang (Dried Pieces of Bean Curd)